Doug Draime
MORE
than the
ALLEY

INTERIOR NOISE PRESS
Austin, Texas USA

More Than The Alley
Copyright © 2012 by Doug Draime

All rights reserved. Printed in the United States of America. No part of this book may be used or reproduced in any manner whatsoever without written permission except in the case of brief quotations embodied in critical articles and reviews.

For order information and current mailing address please visit
www.interiornoisepress.com

Interior Noise Press
Austin, TX

Cover Photo: detail of *Houston Fire Dept.*
Engine Co. No-17
MCH-1927

Book Design by David p Bates

Library of Congress Control Number:

ISBN 978-09816606-6-0
First Edition

for Bill Schute

Contents

Lily And Bob	15
Zoot Sims Crying	19
Glass Factory	20
What I'd Rather Do Than Write Poems For Poets	21
On A Dark Night Across From The Hollywood Cemetery	23
How He Met His First Wife	26
Routine Stop	28
Red's Tavern	30
The First Hooker (or Dead Eyes In Chicago)	31
Vortex Crossing	33
Lincoln Park Zoo	34
Sleeping Without You	35
Near The Canned Goods	36
Protest Organizer	38
Jerry From 13th Street	39
Smoky Afternoon	42
A Flashy Beer Bar In Cincinnati	43
Waiting Tables In Reno	44
Alligator Boots	45

Someday I Will Write A Poem That Will Flood The World	46
Walking On Water	47
Scattered: Configurations Of Matter In Time And Space	49
Jimmy The Toad	51
Resting Aging Bones	52
Burning Bag Of Shit	54
Dreaming Picasso	55
2 p.m.	56
Coming Worlds Apart	57
What She Said On The Phone When She Was Too Drunk To Stop Crying	58
Being Fired From The Sheet Metal Shop By An Ex Lover	60
Memory Of Vincent	61
God Opens A Swiss Bank Account	62
Murray & Mary	63
Steak & Eggs Special	65
19 Straight Whiskeys	66
Warped Amrerican Dream	67

Near The Border Line	69
Finally Realizing	70
Letting The Roses Scream	72
Disneyland	74
The Last *She Said* Poem	76
The Suits Won't Go Away	77
George Raft Movie	79
Third Birthday	80
Lunch At McDonald's	81
Tin Cans	82
Old Homeless Man In St. Francis Hotel Lobby	84
Dream From Motel 6	85
The Poem	86
I Was Told As I Was Sleeping In Mexico	87
After A Strange Conversation With A Member Of Congress	88
More Than The Alley	89
Into The Bleak Abyss Of Night	91
I Didn't Fuck Virginia Woolf	92
Black Sun	93

Friends Of The Ex	94
The True Story Of Noah	95
On The #41 Bus 3 a.m.	96
Entertainment (1920 to present)	97
What She Wrote From Rural America	100
4th & Main	101
Coltrane Mowing The Grass	104
Small Press Editor Gives Advice On How To Get Published In His Magazine	105
Leaving The Coast Of Georgia	106
Ginger Baker	107
The Kid Guru From India	108
Carnival Poem	111
On Elvis Presley's Birthday	112
Sometimes	114
Sincere Foolishness Is Rewarded With Nothing	118
Sally	119
Molly's Place	121
Trip To Nowhere	123
Now That You Are Gone	124

Rural American Saga	125
5 Portraits Of Downtown Los Angeles	127
Boiling Eggs	129
Pretending The Apple Pie Is Fresh	130
Time Travel	131
Bird Watching At Burger King	132
Worker 1943-46	133
Colors And Other Things	134
Coming Full Cycle	135
Living Off The Land	136
Scenes	137
Dream After Reading The 3 Little Pigs To A Bored 4 Year Old On The Beach At Venice	138
What Kind Of Bird Was It	139
Odds	140

The air was soft, the stars so fine, the promise of every cobbled alley so great that I thought I was in a dream.

Jack Kerouac

Lily And Bob

Bob was back
in the corner
by the juke box, his
shotgun propped
up against the
machine. No one
had noticed him
coming in the back-
door. Lily was serving
some rowdies at the
front table. I'd been
watching the Reds kick
the shit outta the
Cubs on the black
& white at the
end of the bar.
And if I hadn't
turned when Jerry
asked for another beer,
I wouldn't have
noticed Bob sitting
there either.
I walked over
and drew Jerry
a draft. Bob was
craning his neck around
trying to get a good
look at Lily. I sat the draft
in front of Jerry
and reached under
the counter for the
.357 and stuck it
under my shirt and
started walking back
to the table.
Bob spotted me coming

and moved his
shotgun, laying
it across the
table, with 2 fingers
resting on the trigger.
He yelled at me,
"This is none of
your concern, Doug.
I just came to
get Lily. Go back
behind the bar
and tend to business."
Lily was
right behind me by
then and I knew
she could see the
bulge of the gun.
"Bob, you need
to take your
fingers off the trigger
and sit the fucking
shotgun back against
the juke box.
And I need you
to do that, now, OK?"
Bob just looked
at me, trying to
stare me down.
The place grew
as quiet as
an empty room.
"I don't want
any trouble with
you, Doug. I
came to get Lily,
like I said."
I could hear

Lily starting to
cry behind me.
"You come in here
with a shotgun
and you don't want
any trouble? I
think you're
a little confused,
man. You need to call it a
night, go home and
sleep if off."
He was just tapping his
fingers on the stock of
the shotgun
near the trigger
and staring at me.
I could feel
Lily moving, as she
touched my
shoulder and stepped
out in front
of me.
She took a couple
steps toward
the table,
haltingly, gently
reaching out
her hand.
"Bob, honey, I'll
leave with you
but you have
to stop this
before someone
gets killed. We
can work
this out, baby.
You don't

want anybody
to get hurt, Bob.
I know
you don't."
Locked on mine,
Bob's eyes moved
slowly away
to Lily's,
his whole
body softening.
He took his hand
off the
shotgun and stood up
his eyes
filling with tears.
Not another word
was spoken
as Bob
began to sob.
Lily had his hand and was
leading him
out the back door.
When I heard
his old pickup start,
I picked up the
shotgun, broke it open
took the shells out
and put them
in my pocket.
Walking back
up to the bar
with the unloaded
weapon, some wise ass played
Lovesick Blues by
Hank Williams
and there was an uproar
of laughter.

Zoot Sims Crying

softly

through the gruesome
plaster walls

there were bloody
screams earlier
of *fuck you, asshole!*
and *I'll kill you, bitch!*

and something horrid
like screaming death, pounding
again and again

on the unyielding linoleum floor

but now there is only jagged
laughter, the clanging of glasses

and Zoot Sims his sax
crying *Autumn Leaves*

softly

through the gruesome
plaster walls

so softly

it breaks my heart

again

Glass Factory

For several months
every night
my grandfather
would fall asleep
sitting in front of the television
after dinner, which he would
just pick at and
never finish. Every night
he would
wake with a start
between 8 and 8:30
his eyes blinking
open and shut
rapidly
several times
and scream
Watch out, Frank, the goddamn
sheet is slipping
Referring to the 8 by 12 foot sheet
of glass that fell from a crane
killing one of his crew at the glass factory
where he'd worked
for over 30 years as a foreman.
I don't remember when
he stopped screaming
nor do I recall him
ever
mentioning watching
his friend practically
sliced in two and bleeding
to death
in his arms.

What I'd Rather Do Than Write Poems For Poets

I'd rather
write jokes
for a stand up
comic

eating a corn beef
on rye

reaching for
the brown
mustard

drunk out of
his gourd

at Cantor's
Deli at 1:30
in the morning

I'd rather watch
Dr. Strangenuts
banging the

stuffing out
of Lois Lane

while Superman
jacks off

in a
phone

booth

I'd rather see
little Cindy

from Louisville
(now Victoria Starburst)

topless up on a
revolving stage

doing the

goddamn

hokey-

pokey

On A Dark Night Across From The Hollywood Cemetery

She threw a large half-full
Lysol spray can at me.
It hit me under the
left eye
and cut me open.
Her 5 year old daughter
came out from
the back bedroom
and stood behind
her mother
in the doorway
wide eyed
terrified from all our
yelling
and the blood dripping
down my face.
I told her
to go back
in the bedroom
that everything would be OK
that it was
just about over. I was so
drunk I barely felt
the gash and the large
mouse that was
forming
under my eye. Her mother
who was drunker than me
abruptly sat down on the
couch, still half-ass yelling
at me. She had
stopped throwing things
so I picked up
a paper napkin
from the coffee table
sat down

in a chair across from her
and pressed it against
my wound.
I sat for a moment
trying to apply
enough pressure
to stop the
bleeding.
When I looked up
her daughter was
standing
in front of me
handing me a wet washcloth
and a band aid
her beautiful blue eyes
still as big as moons. I looked over
at her mother
but she had passed out
on the couch.
I smiled and took
the washcloth and cleaned out
the cut, dried it
with another napkin
and stuck on the band aid.
She told me
in a matter of fact way
her voice only
slightly shaky
that she
was going back to bed
and if I was going to
leave
please cover up her mother
and turn out
the light
when I left.
I thanked her for the

washcloth and band aid
and reached out
and touched her on the arm
telling her
I wouldn't leave
till her mother felt
better in the morning.
She just pulled away from me gently, smiling
and said it was OK
that the other
men had just left her sleeping on
the couch, or sometimes the floor.
Nodding at me, she turned and walked
back down
the hallway
into her room
and closed
the door
quietly.

How He Met His First Wife

"it was
so quiet
you could
hear a
cockroach
pissing
on your
underwear,"
he said.
then he
looked
at me &
shook his
head
sighing
as if
bearing
up under
the weight
of all
human
perversity

he took another blast of whiskey

"suddenly
she just
started
screaming &
smashing
the empty
beer bottles
against
the kitchen
wall
spewing

out all
kinds of hate
& foulness.
it didn't
take
long
to dawn
on me
that I'd
stuck my
dick in the
wrong
go-go
dancer."

Routine Stop

The cops stopped
and had to inform me I
was on Grant street
in Santa Monica.

"Well, kiss my ass,"
I joked with one of the cops.
"The last thing I remember
I was smoking a joint
at a friend's house in Silverlake."

That's when I had to *re-learn*
that you don't joke
with the cops. Or for that matter
you can't be honest
with cops about "illegal
drugs" or anything else that
might be held up to serious debate.

Part of what I said was the truth
and the other part was just
a joke. I knew I wasn't in Silverlake
anymore and I was quite aware
I was staggering some down Grant street
having lost count of how many
beers I'd consumed since I'd
left Silverlake. So I
pretended I was more messed-up
than I actually was, just to sort of, well
fuck with 'em.

"You trying to be a wise ass? You
just look like a drunk hippie to me,"
said the other cop, with a potent dose of venom.

"I wasn't talking to you. I was talking

to your partner," I replied, without
turning to look at him.

I knew that was a mistake the
instant it came out of my mouth
but I couldn't help myself.

He grabbed me from behind
turned me around
pushed me against the squad
car and turned me around again.
"Spread eagle, you piece of shit,"
he snarled at me and then patted
me down hard as he punched my ribs
and cuffed me.

"This was just a routine stop, you
asshole, until you shot-off your
fucking mouth," he said grabbing
the back of my arms and leading
me to the back seat.

The Santa Monica cop-shop/lockup
was much nicer than the Hollywood
Precinct that I had become accustomed
to. There was a color tv in the walkway
separating the cells and access to
vending machines of soda, candy and
cigarettes.

The next morning when they cut me
loose I left a note for the cop that roughed
me up. *"Hey, Paul, I was really only
joking. But cops like you are the reason
people hate and fear cops. Maybe food
for thought, maybe not. Love, Doug."*

Red's Tavern

Pete's stab wounds
were a badge of honor.
Pulling his beer stained
Dodger t-shirt up
showing me
a 5 inch scar
across his huge
beer belly.

That's something, man
I said.

He jumped up from his stool
turned around and
with both hands
pulled his t-shirt
up to the back of his neck

revealing a large, imbedded
nasty looking gush
in the middle of his back
clear down to
the cheeks of his fat ass.

He turned around with a goofy
drunken smile on his face
pulling his shirt down. "The ex done
that with a broken beer bottle the
night she left and went to Tucson.
They say I lost 4 pints of blood."

That's something, man
I said again and bought him a
beer for *that* one.

The First Hooker
(or Dead Eyes In Chicago)

I was 19
on an all night
binge of coffee
and Vick's
Benzedrine
inhalers,
sitting in the coffee shop
of the Greyhound
bus station
on Dearborn.
I was watching the
dead eyes of
the waitress, arguing
with the dead eyes
of the cook.
There were 2 limp-wrist faggots
cruising the stools
for a hunk
of meat
with their cold dead eyes.
A dead eyed cop stood
by the door
to the street talking to
a pretty blond
hooker and
her eyes were alive and bright blue.

My hophead friend, Roger
from Evanston
rode the El in everyday
on his
parent's money
to score, and he always
bought the coffee.
Roger watched too, looking her

up and down with his
own junk dead eyes; my eyes–
deadest of all
getting an entrancing stare from
her alive, bright blue eyes
while I
rubbed myself to an erection
under the counter .

Vortex Crossing

I counted the steps of my childhood home
several years after it was sold and broken
up into apartments. I stood in front of the
house and counted 9 steps. I was 36 at
the time. Remembering at 16, laying drunk
one night on the top step like a dead alley
cat. I remembered, distinctly, waking just
before dawn and carefully counting 13 steps,
including the one I threw up on.

Lincoln Park Zoo

the biggest, badest-ass male lion
in the place
won't take
his eyes off me

i am eating fresh roasted peanuts
and drinking
a bottle of
orange Nehi

sitting on a bench
15 feet
from him
in his caged domain

and i won't
take my eyes
off him either
as 3 females gently lick his ears

and sniff his ass
like it was a sweet smelling fresh orchid

our eyes lock
and i envy that bad-ass motherfuckering lion

but i know if push came to shove

he'd rip me to blood and shank

for my peanuts and soda

while his adoring harem calmly wait for what is left of me

Sleeping Without You
for Carol

I toil with these damp sheets
in your absence
Hello to Newport Beach
Hello to Moe's
Hello to our spot
      by the
black driftwood
down the South Beach in a cave
calling our names
through the mist of sea
Hello to the woman poet whose
name escapes me but her poems
of rage still rattle and shake
      my being
from the rocky coast of Oregon
Hello to the mock opulence of
the Shilo Inn and the bed
we shared the sheets soaked
with our cum the sheets soaked with
our divine and filthy sweat
soaked with the sea from our bodies
drenched in our spirits
Hello to the grains of sand the
universe between your
      naked toes
      as you walk along the surf
Hello to you
Hello to you
I woke thinking of you
my sheets damp and musty

Near The Canned Goods

There was a
little blonde
headed kid
running down
the aisle
of
Safeway
crying
followed in
storming
pursuit
was his
raging
and
screaming
mother.

I handed
him
a can of
baked beans
as he ran
by.
"Here, kid,"
I said
"drive this
through her
heart."

At the check-out
stand
paying for
my beer and smokes
I heard
the ignorant cunt

yelling in agony like
a stuck
pig.

Protest Organizer

Century City in
1967, or 8, very stoned
to protest
Lyndon Johnson's
speech. We were
among the
crowd the cops
were pushing back
and yelling at us
to *cease and desist*.
She took my hand
and placed it
between her legs
up her lily white
sun dress. When the
speech was over
she drove me home
to my place on
Lexington in Hollywood.
And she jacked me
off and I came in her mouth.
When I finally got
out of the car, she
insisted that I take not
one but *two* Stop The War
t-shirts.

Jerry From 13th Street

There was the perpetual
Pall Mall cigarette
hanging from his mouth.
And he was always
picking on kids
smaller and younger
than him.
His wooden leg and
foot clanged and
rattled as
he walked. It had happened
when he was twelve
trying to jump
into a boxcar
of a moving train. Two of
his friends had
made it, one chickened
out. Jerry miscalculated
his run and came up
short, reaching for the edge
of the boxcar's
open door, and the motion
of the train pulled
him under. Somehow he was
able to keep one leg
free, but the rest of his body
slipped under the
steel wheels. Every kid
in the neighborhood
was afraid
of him, every kid but me.
To me he was just a pimple-faced
fat kid with a wooden leg.
One day he was coming
down the alley
with a couple of his friends. I was

fifteen, but already well over
6 feet and a solid 175 pounds.
He and his friends were
maybe sixteen, overweight
and a couple of inches shorter.
They were all three smoking
as they passed.
Jerry sneered, flipping his Pall Mall
at me. It hit my t-shirt and
bounced to the ground. They
stopped and were laughing
calling me a
dumb-ass and a son-of-a-bitch.
I didn't say a word, I just
quickly walked right up
into their faces. They were
startled and
took a step backwards.
My uncle had lost a leg in WW2
and I knew what the
weakest part
of a wooden leg was. I was an
arm's distance away
from Jerry, who was
lighting another cigarette,
still sneering. I turned my body
slightly and kicked
his wooden knee.
He seemed to fall instantaneously
tumbling over
to his left
in a barrage of yelling and
clanging. His friend, who was
standing to the right
of him, took a step forward
as if he was going
to take a punch at me. I swung

wildly, hitting him
somewhere around the
collarbone, and I was winding up
another when he turned
and ran down the alley. The other
kid was faster
passing his friend easily.
I watched them run
out of the alley to the sidewalk.
Jerry was still yelling and crying
on the ground, begging me
to help him up. I told him I wouldn't
help him, but that I would
call his parents
when I got home. I left him laying
there crying, as I jumped
over the next door neighbor's fence.
I walked across
their backyard into mine, went into
my house
called Jerry's parents and
told his mother that
he had had an accident and
was in the alley. My dad
overheard the conversation
and asked
what was going on.
I told him I had just kicked
the ass of Jerry from over
on 13th street. He laughed
and said it was
about time someone
cleaned that bastard's plow.
That was the first time
I got drunk
with my old man,
but far from
the last.

Smoky Afternoon

I smoke a joint and
watch Judge Judy.
But I gotta turn the
old gal off. I've been
watching her too many
afternoons, her and
Judge Joe, and smoking weed.
They're both starting to look like
W.E.B. DuBois
on a bad day
when he was
well over 90 years old, maybe
sitting in a dim-lit
room in Ghana nodding off
after reading Little
Orphan Annie
and other stupid lies
from white capitalists
in America

A Flashy Beer Bar In Cincinnati

chips of refined
azure stones
imbedded
in the
mahogany
bar rail.
it was the last
and only
thing i
remember
before i
hit the floor.
and then the taste
of sawdust
a terrible pain
in my head
and lights
fading to a
dull sudden
blackness.
the woman the
fight
started over
was long gone
and the
cops were
unreasonable
assholes.

Waiting Tables In Reno

40 years ago
she left him
while he was
getting his
leg blown off
in Nam.

Now,
here she was
waiting tables
in Reno– not even
recognizing him–
after she almost
fell over his
prosthetic leg.

"Keep your legs
under the table, sir,
I could've fallen and
broken something."

Alligator Boots

The Ku Klux Klan used to
ride down Main Street
in my hometown
on horses
with their white sheets
and hoods
in 4th of July parades
up until the 1950's.
I remember one year
my grandfather, not normally
a drinker, was lit up
on some beers
and ran up to one of
the men on the horses
and called out
the name *Harry*.
And the man leaned down
in acknowledgment.
I heard my grandfather yell,
"I knew it was you, from those
shit kickin' alligator boots of yours."
They were both laughing
as my grandfather jumped up a little
and pulled Harry's hood
from his head.
My grandfather ran
back to my dad
and me on the sidewalk
still laughing with hood in hand.
Harry continued down the street
on his horse, seemingly unaffected
by the exposure. In fact he appeared
to relish in it, smiling,
his head held high, and waving proudly
at his neighbors
who were calling out to him.

Someday I Will Write A Poem That Will Flood The World

And I will own all the
arks, boats, ships,
rafts, and canoes,
and tug boats, ferries–
all forms of water transportation.

People will have to come
to me for their means
of survival.

The stubborn and destitute ones
will drown in my poem
sinking to the bottom
screeching like anchors on
rusty
chains.

The rest of humanity will plead
for cut-rate discounts. But fuck them.
I'll make them pay out
the ass. No rainbows
this time.

Walking On Water

I walked into the Wabash river
up to my waist
fully clothed
drunk out of my mind at 16. I thought
for a moment there
that I could really
walk on water.
My friends on the bank
of the sand bar, screaming
at me to
get my ass out
that someone
had called the cops.
But 12 bottles
of Miller High Life
and a half pint
of Jim Beam
had set me on a mission,
sent me over the wobbling edge
into some kind of insane spiritual probing
of elated intoxication and power and
uncontrollable fits of laughter. Kenny threw
a rock that hit the water
just to the left of me. Then Vic
threw an empty beer bottle
that I had to duck
to avoid from smashing into my head.
And I just laughed and
laughed and laughed. I have yet to see
the moon and stars
quite as beautiful and mind blowing
as they were
on that night. And I looked up
and laughed hysterically at them, too
just before the cops got there
andI made them walk into the river to get me.

I laughed and prophesied their doom
all the way to the county lockup.
But the view of the night sky from the
barred jail cell window wasn't
quite the same.

Scattered: Configurations Of Matter In Time And Space

Scattered in the pouch of a cross-eyed kangaroo at the St. Louis
>   Zoo
Scattered across the melting sands of time
Scattered unrecognizable by those no one knows or wants to know
Scattered for the sake of the mass gathering of the betrayal's blade
Scattered on the balcony by jacking off voyeurs calling themselves
>   lovers

Scattered in wheat fields by drunken CEO's of unbelievably corrupt
>   corporations
Scattered on the desks of detectives in the Missing Persons department
Scattered inside coffins in Little Italy stuffed with homemade sausages
Scattered in dusty, mournful, crowded rooms of those who think
>   they are alive
Scattered in the words of unread suicide notes

Scattered among the ruins of disillusioned illusions and other tricks
>   of ancient mind
Scattered by beautiful and suntanned naked women wearing NY
>   baseball caps
Scattered on the banks of deadly industrial waste streams, where
>   nothing can live
Scattered like confectionary sugar over the unmarked graves in
>   Nam and Iraq
Scattered in the brain cells of memory in an Alzheimer trance

Scattered without any rhyme, reason. or compassionate order
Scattered down the first base line at Dodger Stadium in a pouring
>   thunder storm
Scattered and mixed in with the star dust in the reeking gutters of
>   desolation row
Scattered and diseased in the smoldering ovens at Buchenwald

Scattered outside the walls of Jericho

Scattered in the men's room at a bomb making plant next to McDonalds
Scattered in the humor and dissident barbs of a George Carlin routine

Scattered in all the movies that play reel to reel in our minds lifetime after lifetime
Scattered in the dust and elitism of City Lights bookstore
Scattered in the pumping air and striving of the human heart

Jimmy The Toad

They said I was
babbling incoherently
and swinging at
anyone
who got within
5 feet of me.
No one in the bar
at the time
could handle
the situation.
And Maxine ran
next door to
Ray's Market
and got my friend
Jimmy the Toad.
All I know
is when I woke up
in the hospital
with a broken nose
and 2 cracked ribs
Jimmy was leaning
over me
crying
and apologizing
for using a little
too much force,
offering me
a bowl of
orange sherbet.

Resting Aging Bones

I really was attempting to
pay attention
the best I could, to focus
on the young poet
reading his poems.
I hadn't sleep well
in several days, my legs
aching from all
the walking
I was doing looking for
some kind of work.
48, let me clue you in,
is no age to be
without income and
nowhere to go
to call your own.

I needed a place to sit down
and rest for awhile.
The poet was trying
to be poetic, his poems
full of run of the mill
similes, that contained
no fortitude
of spirit, or passion.
And I'm sorry to say
I fell into
a deep sleep.
I don't know for how long
but a college coed
stinking of patchouli oil and
sweat, shook me awake.
"You're snoring. That's really
rude," she said.
I looked up and the poet
was glaring

at me.
All 20 eyes of the 10 people
sitting in the
folding chairs
were glaring at me.

I said, nodding at the poet,
"Sorry about that. Good luck
with those similes, kid."
And I got up and walked
out of the bookstore
and down the street
to the nearest bar
where I ordered
a small pitcher of beer
with $3 of
my last $10.
I found a table in the corner
sat down
and immediately
fell back to sleep.
Karen, the bartender
was kind enough to let me
sleep till
closing time.

Burning Bag Of Shit

She found the last 50 poems I wrote
in my notebook, cut them out
put them through her office shredder
twice: once lengthwise and then
width-wise. She told me all
of this, as she was standing
screaming and crying on the stoop
in front of my apartment, with the pieces of
my poems in a small paper bag. She
took out *my* Zippo from her ass-tight
jean pocket, lit the bag, waited for it
to get going good, before she
dropped it at my feet and turned
still crying and ran to her car. I watched
her drive away and walked back into
my apartment, letting the bag of words
burn like a bag of shit on Halloween.
I made a cup of strong black tea and sat down
at the kitchen table with a new notebook
and I started another poem...
just for fucking spite.

Dreaming Picasso

I was running down
the alley from the cops.
I was so drunk I forget
for what.
I ducked into the back
room of a bar
in the Bronx or
Brooklyn
(who knows which, I was
drunk and dreaming).
But Picasso was
already in there, shit faced
himself, hiding from
Dora Maar.
I quickly held my finger up to my lips
because I knew
he'd start rattling on loudly
about her atrocities.
He smiled, though, and
got quiet for a moment.
But he couldn't take not getting it out at all
and he started mumbling
things
I couldn't hear in
rapid-fire Spanish.
His luminescent black
eyes big as mud pies.

2 p.m.

He said he'd lost his mind

many years before

and that he was still looking

for it in all the same, insane places

He pushed the small pitcher

of beer he'd bought me closer

I poured a glass and held it up

for a toast, to bums and poets

I said, touching his double shot of

Jim Beam with my glass of draft

He made a face "I don't know about

poets, fuck poets, but here's

to bums who have lost their minds"

Coming Worlds Apart

We had little in common
(except we both loved sex)
She used heroin
I smoked pot
She loved disco
I invented the term *disco sucks*
She was a rich young widow
I was a poor young starving writer hanging on the edge
She was full of bourgeois culture
I lived a counter-cultural lifestyle
She liked fancy restaurants
I was a bean and spaghetti man
She had a Doctorate in Comparative Literature from UCLA
I barely got through 2 semesters on the G.I. Bill
    at Los Angeles City College
She believed in the political process and voted
I didn't vote and thought politics was a cancer and
    could solve nothing

She was reading William James, Robert Frost and
    Susan Sontag
I was reading Louis-Ferdinard Celine, Henry Miller
    and LeRoi Jones
She bought things
I gave away things
She thought the Black Panther Party were criminals
I considered them heroes
She liked movie musicals
I hated them
She drank Southern Comfort on the rocks
I drank Eastside beer the cheapest I could find
She drove a Lincoln convertible
I took buses and cabs
We both loved sex
We got high and had sex and smoked cigarettes
(but not the same brand)

What She Said On The Phone When She Was Too Drunk To Stop Crying

Her face still haunts me
with its near
perfection
a cross between
Greta Garbo and
Grace Kelly.
But her heart
was ravaged
by bitterness
by dysfunction.
Her betrayals calculated
attacks just for
the hell of it.
Her constant deceptions
and games
destroyed any feelings
I had had for her
and I sent her packing
only a couple months
after she'd moved in.
Hollywood wanted to
make her
a star, but she chose
being a whore
instead: a dominatrix
with leather, chains
and elaborate whips.
She got most of her trade
through the personal ads
in the Los Angeles Free Press
She was doing 2 or 3 freaks a day.
And in the face of
each one, she saw the eyes
of her
drunk and abusive father.

And with each lash
of the whip, she thought
death to you, you fucking bastard
her bitter, salty tears
flooding the wounds
like embalming fluid.
Death to you, you letch,
you drunk.

Being Fired From The Sheet Metal Shop By An Ex Lover

Hammering the tin flat
I could feel her eyes
watching, traveling up
and down my body
from the office overlooking
the machines.
She walked down the stairs
into the work area
with my check in her beautiful hand.
Her thick black hair shiny
and pulled back
tightly into a bun.
The sheet of tin was held
snug in the automatic vise
as I continued to hammer.
But then I felt her closer
smelling the *Tabu* she wore
feeling the heat of her body.
I looked up wiping
my brow.
Her cold, dark eyes slamming
into my mine:
"We're gonna have to let you go."
I pointed down at my gym bag.
"I took my stuff outta my locker this morning,
I figured this was coming."
She didn't say a word, just handed me
my check, turned and walked away
in her tight white mini-skirt.
As she walked back up the wooden stairs
a couple of guys on the other machines
grabbed their crotches
one stuck his tongue out intimating
cunnilingus.

Memory Of Vincent

He had everything down
to an exact science,
he said, as he arranged
his sparse belongings
in his cardboard dwelling
to make room for me.
There was a stack of
newspapers in the corner
and a picture of a little girl
in a small silver frame
sitting on top.
It was a snug fit but there was
more room in there than I had thought.
Once I was in and turned to face out
I noticed a large backpack
and a small Coleman stove neatly packed
in a corner by the entrance.
He pulled out a pint of cheap whiskey
that we'd pooled our money to buy.
We shared the bottle
talking about the hostility
of downtown L.A. cops
but nothing about ourselves;
Nixon was president
and we both hated him.
The rest of the time we sat quietly drinking and
watching the nine-to-fivers
drive down Hill Street for home
without a bit of envy.

God Opens A Swiss Bank Account

I never expected the
burnt offerings. I didn't
care whether it was a
goat or a
14 year old virgin. I
was in it for
the money: the gold
and silver coins, land deeds,
trust funds,
resalable mutual bonds
placed at the altar
of my feet.
Must you bring slaughter
and idolatry into
the matter?
I can't use your ATM cards,
too many numbers
to remember.

Murray & Marie

I wasn't sure he had both
oars in the water, but he was
my only connection.
He was *Murray The
Bennie Man*.
He lived in a room above
a hardware store on Clark.
There was always an
invitation to stay
after I scored. There was
a *hot number* next door, a speed
and sex freak named Marie
who liked to
*fuck and suck and do
masturbation shows.*
Nearly every time I was there
he'd get up from
his filthy bed and creep over
like an institutionalized retard and
tap on the wall, giggling.
I drank his battery acid Maxwell House
coffee and dropped
a few of the pills.
Murray would ramble on
about this *female*, as he walked back to
his bed to lay down.
After a couple minutes, he'd suddenly
jump up and be over at the wall
again, tapping and giggling.
This routine would last for 15 or
20 minutes.
I never saw Marie
in the dozen or so times I
was there. She was
there, though, if not in the flesh
definitely in the mind

and the dick.
In fact, every time he'd talk about her,
describing her sexual appetite
in dirty detail,
I'd get
aroused and
have to leave to
cruise the bars in Old Town
for a woman
any woman.

Steak & Eggs Special

3:30 a.m. breakfast at Norm's:
$3.95 steak & eggs special
best deal in east hollywood

a girl in a leather dress
a stranger
sits down across from me in the booth

you havin' the special? she asks
yeah   i say
i am too   she says   but adds:
separate checks ok?
ok   i agree

then she takes her shoe off
& gently puts
a slender
black-nyloned foot
against my crotch

19 Straight Whiskeys

If I would have been
there at the Chelsea Hotel
drinking
with Dylan Thomas
the night
they drove him away
in an ambulance
I would have told him all
the fame and booze
was mutilating
his soul.
The hangers-on, writers, editors,
other drunks, leeches, and the women
spreading their
nylon legs.
All of them killing him
or watching him die
and doing nothing to stop it.
They say he said on that night
"I've had 18 straight whiskeys. I think
that's the record."
I would have told him all that shit was killing him.
I would have cut him off at 9 whiskeys.
But then again, maybe I might've
kept my nose out
of his business and matched him
drink for drink,
going on and beating his record
with 19 and
leaving with one of the
women before
the ambulance arrived.

Warped American Dream

No one in my
home town knew
the connection
between
Little Richard
and
Norman Mailer

I would listen
to *Long Tall Sally*
and
the flip side
Jenny, Jenny
on my 45 RPM
locked up in
my room
for days
while I read
Mailer's *White Negro*

My old man and grandparents
wanted to have me
committed
and my chicken-shit friends
bad mouthed
me behind
my back
because I
listened to
nigger music
and read
strange books

Sex/ drinking/
reading and
rock 'n roll

were the only
things that
filled me with
life and
wonderment

Everything else
was dead
and false

I was surrounded
by bigots
and the ignorant
even those my
age whose
spirits and
possibilities
had been
blotted or
wiped out
somehow
or maybe
they were born
that way:
*poor white
trash*
the mutated
off-shoots
of the warped
American
dream

Near The Border Line

The motel was on the
outskirts of a town
from a drunken
John Houston movie.

I remember the exact placement
of the 5th of Johnny Walker Red
sitting next to the glasses
on the night stand but I
don't remember her name.

Her eyes were light blue and like dimming
bar lights, flickering over my
shoulders, always looking at the
graying adobe.

I kept the tv on and I must have
rolled 10 joints.

She liked it from behind bent over the
metal desk.
Those lovely shadow-eyes blinking on and off at
the walls.
She never smiled once and gave me
one word answers to
my questions, only looking at me
when I turned away.
She didn't even look up
when I paid her $20 more than she
said she was worth.

Finally Realizing

48 yrs after
his death
he was 24
I was 12–
you do the
math–
I am finally
realizing
I'll *never* be
another
James Dean
This news will
be a
disappoint-
ment
to my
deceased
father
who was an
Indiana
socialist
who thought
Dean was the
only *true*
artist ever in
American movie
culture
Sorry, dad
that my
biggest
acting role
was in a
film that was
picketed &
shut down
2 days after

it opened
at a
Japanese
movie
theater in
South Central L.A.
for "exploitation
of the people"

Letting The Roses Scream

I am out on my back deck again with
the dog, cats; a bottle of beer in my hand
the radio playing
and the noise of my hyperactive neighbor
who is always banging around
on something in his back yard.
I dis him to my wife and whoever will
listen. Though, actually, he's really
not a bad sort: an environmentalist and a former
punk rocker.
And when I see him
he chatters on about his therapy
the benefits of yoga, saving the environment
and offers me marijuana laced brownies
with an innocent puppy dog charm
that takes me in. At these times I have to
remember that he is like a hyperactive
child, a compulsive *motherfucker*
who is forever doing something very *loudly* on the other side
of the fence I have to put up with.
This afternoon I am trying to focus on some jazz
over the radio, some old Gerry Mulligan and admiring the
beautiful red roses my wife planted. Suddenly, all hell
breaks loose on the other side of the fence as he starts up
some kind of drill or jack hammer like a magpie
being strangled. The dog begins to bark
and I do believe I hear the flowers screaming
over the pitch of it all, screaming at me to do something:
climb over the fence and
crack this imbecile over the head with a ball bat
cut him up in oblong pieces with a machete
blow his former punk-rocking balls off with my
unregistered handgun.
The last time I listened to screaming flowers was
25 years ago in L.A.
they were 7-foot tall sunflowers and I was crazy drunk
in my back yard in Echo Park shooting at

a couple of Chicano kids who had tried to break
into my house on Christmas day. Thanks to a
sudden moment of clarity, I fired 2 shots from my .38
above their heads as they hauled ass over my
high knotty pine fence.
The cops came and I was hauled off to the
downtown lockup for 4 days, charged with disturbing
the peace and discharging a firearm inside the county limits.
So today I let the roses scream; but if the cantaloupes
or tomatoes start shooting off
their mouths, I'm going to have to climb over
my fence and fuck the guy up.

Disneyland

Mickey Mouse
sold out
in 1939
when he
pawned
his
tug boat
to Hitler
to pull
cargo ships full of
dead
bodies
stuffed inside
thousands
of Volkswagens
like marinating
sardines.

They say
Walt is
frozen
somewhere.
I most
respectfully
suggest
someone
sneak in and
place
a good sized
space
heater
next to him
in
his ice tomb
to keep
him

dead.
He's done enough
for the
world.

The Last *She Said* Poem

She said *all* my
writing was full of *rage*
and morose
and that I just used
being a writer
as an excuse for
being a drunk and
an asshole.

I was blind drunk again and she
was driving. We were headed
down Fountain Avenue
in Hollywood, in her mini-
Volvo station wagon.

I attempted unsuccessfully
to push her from
the car.

Last I heard she moved back
to New York City
and was working for a
lesbian stage actress
who paid her in
sex and cocaine.

I'm still an asshole but I stopped
        drinking.

The Suits Won't Go Away

I've seen these *Suits*
with dead faces
since I was a
kid. I remember
closing my eyes tight
after looking
at an insurance salesman
or a preacher (how do
you tell the difference?)
and praying he would not
be there
when I opened them.
I still do it at times with
CEO's in their
designer suits and generals
in battle dress: death arrayed
in ribbons across
their breast.
I still shut my eyes tight
at morticians and talk show hosts
and lying politicians
with a hint of color in their
Porky Pig neckties.
Not to say, though, that all
men who have worn or who wear
suits are on my shit list.
Camus looked fantastic in a suit.
Presley wore suits with an unmistakable cool.
Miles and Coltrane and Kenneth Patchen
wore suits.
And Einstein wore a black rumpled suit
with impeccable class.
I admire men like *that* who happened to
have worn suits!
Men who have something to sell
other than

war, mind control and
spiritual stagnation.
I know the *Suits* will not go away
no matter how long
I close my eyes and pray.
It's been the same since
the white race rose to power.
The Huns were *Suits*, and down
the line, Hitler.
Many of our leaders imitate him
wearing his *Suit* of death:
perfect fit, no tailoring
needed.

George Raft Movie

I always wanted to walk
into a restaurant
or a nightclub
like in an old George Raft movie
where there's
a beautiful hat check girl
and I know her by name. Well, I more
than *know* her
having had carnal relations
with her
the night before
doggie style as she
bent over the hat check counter inside
where all the hats sat
like bored and reluctant voyeurs.
Anyhow, I walk in, say *hi* to her
she could be a Roxy
or a Sylvia. She's in a tight red dress
cut up both sides to
her thighs. I am immediately hard and
all I want to do is fuck her again
bent over the counter.
She smiles and her big brown eyes
sweep down my body
like a very hot breeze.
And her eyes linger on my crotch
as she tells me I am welcome
to come back after closing time
to pick up the hat
I left behind.

Third Birthday

He mumbles at the ground. His white
mane of hair like a stringy damp blanket
over his head. 15 years on the streets.
His wife and children living
with his ex-best friend
in Pasadena.
Two cardboard TV boxes are his home
in back of a garment factory
on 6th street. I share the bottle with him
on the lawn of the downtown library. He's
coherent for several moments,
recalling his youngest daughter at 3 years old.
The last time he saw her she was playing
with a doll he had bought for her birthday.
He starts to shake and cry and looks off
down the street. I sit there awhile and finally
get up and walk off, leaving him there with his memories
and the half empty bottle of rot gut.

Lunch At McDonald's

Everybody thinks
they discovered me.
Pride kills deeper
than bullets. An aging
poet working in the
back of a newspaper
counting and stacking
tons of newsprint.
None of my fellow workers
at the table
(all at least 25 years younger)
even read the
newspaper they work for, not to mention
poetry.
Between bites
of my double cheeseburger,
I say that my poems
usually don't rhyme. A couple
people at the table nod.
I'm sure it answers their
silent question
as to why I'm not famous.

Tin Cans
In Memory Of Ray Charles

I was 15 or 16
when you were helped
from the stage in
Indianapolis, mumbling
incoherently and later
arrested for narcotics possession
partying at the Claypool Hotel.
That night I was only 100 miles away
in Vincennes
playing *What'd I Say* at full volume
on my 45 RPM
using 2 large empty potato chip cans
as conga drums.
Dazed, and a little messed up
from some Thunderbird wine I had
smuggled up to my room
and more than a little bummed-out
over having missed seeing you.
Halfway through the song my grandfather
flung the door open
yelling at me to turn that nigger shit down.
The next day after I heard about your bust
I came home from school,
got out my cans and played you again
at full volume, finishing off the wine.
No one was home and I played that song
at least 15 times.
That afternoon changed me forever, man.
But the wine, with only a little food on my stomach
made me sleepy and I took a long nap.
I had a dream I'd made it to your concert–
that you played your full set *very* conscious
with 3 encores and you were not arrested afterwards.
And the next morning you were given the key to the city

and a lavish gala dinner
put on by the Indiana chapter of the KKK,
bowing and scraping at your feet.

Old Homeless Man In St. Francis Hotel Lobby

I could see
it was all
he could do
to keep
from crying
and I
kept expecting
his lower lip
to begin trembling
and sobs
to shake
his bent body.
But he was dignified,
holding himself erect
as he talked to the
nightly news;
cursing   raving
at the television
over the
war.

Dream From Motel 6

Drunk, and having no memory
how I got there:
the only passenger
in a front seat of an
out of control Greyhound bus

A 300 pound man supposed to be driving
black hair slicked back
dressed in an Elvis
blue sequined jumpsuit
and with white boots
slumped/ passed out
or dead
over the steering wheel
which was
bouncing in tiny zigzag patterns
pressed with the weight of his body
speeding down
Market Street
headed pall mall
for the Wharf and
off and over the end
the Pacific devouring
the Elvis impersonator
the 5 ton machine, and me

When I woke up
I was drenched in sweat
and there were
skid marks
from my feet
deep into the mattress
but I was alive, and ravenously
hungry for deep fried shrimp
cole slaw and several
ice cold beers

The Poem

I know I have
succeeded
in *this*
because I have
failed at everything
else. Just ask
my ex-wife
ask any phony poet of
flowers and cheap
reflections.

They will tell you
I have failed
miserably at life
and poetry.

Ask my teachers
ask my employers.
Ask the cops
ask the IRS.
Go ahead ask the U.S. Army.

Request my file from the F.B.I.
Question the
would-be assassins of
my soul.
They will all be in agreement.
nodding their heads like retarded sheep.

I Was Told As I Was Sleeping In Mexico

There was
light from the
setting sun
over my left
shoulder dancing
on my
bare sunburned body.
The TV set was muted
on the news
coverage of the war
and my body
started twitching in some
kind of violent seizure.
It lasted for several
minutes, until
the TV was
turned off
and my body
abruptly fell into
the soft, deep
breathing
of a sleeping
contented
baby boy.

After A Strange Conversation With A Member Of Congress

You give me your schedule and
I'll give you mine and we'll stand
on the hill overlooking the concentration
camp. You born without feet
under the American flag in
your child molesting grandfather's
house in East Jersey: hair like
insane human meat shrieking
in the hell of pity. The shadows
                        dank, reeking
of the history of other
                        feet-less souls.
You say you've read Kafka and the Bible
and walked on burning coals.
It's a way to cope
                lying to yourself.
But everybody knows
you ain't got no feet.

More Than The Alley

I fought in alleys as a kid
in the small town alleys
of Vincennes and the city, steel-
soot alleys of
Pittsburgh, for no other reason
than I had to fight. It was something
unavoidable, destined.
I won the majority of them
which means nothing. I could have
just as well lost most and it would not
have mattered.
It wasn't the winning
or the losing, that had nothing
to do with it
just as words often have nothing
to do with poetry.
It was more than
the battle, the alley
or the crowds
taking perverse delight
in the blood flying from adolescent faces
cracked bones and the possibility
of serious injury.
Something, some pure rage inside prodded
me on and I was always
astonished after
to find myself reasonably intact
having come through one of the most
dangerous
kinds of human interchange.
There was never a fight
in which I didn't
shake from a sickening deep gut fear
my hands trembling like
a dumb unconsecrated nun.

The swallowing of my fear was like
choking down razor blades but
I would take a deep breath, swallow
and swing hard.

Into The Bleak Abyss Of Night

Memory of the egg of fossils
in the DNA the stabbing
blade of the betrayer:
The forever bleeding
human heart skin
of the snake. They say
photographs of a dinosaur
triceratops to be exact
taken 80 million
years ago or
15 thousand years ago what
does it matter? Memory
replaces everything lost
in memory. African slave
traders murdering
the weaker Santa
Monica boardwalk
of 1944 a pink suit
spattered with blood
lies told to an
ex-lover now
dead. Assembled in a crevice just a
sliver in the mind an
image brought to
the forefront a memory of a violent night 10 years ago.
Smashing through the window with your fists
black birds across the road on the wire singing a mournful
song into
the bleak abyss of night.

I Didn't Fuck Virginia Woolf

I had a dream I
slept with Virginia Woolf
but I couldn't keep
my erection.
She didn't help matters
any, just laying
there reading the
London Times. So we
decided to
to go to sleep.
And in the middle
of the
night
I had a wet dream
about Henry Miller's
second wife
June. I was embarrassed
because I woke
Virginia, but she was
gentle and
empathic
asking me to describe
in vivid detail
June's voluptuous body
and nasty
mind.

Black Sun

The death bone
worm knows
your name
can smell
your rot
before you are
pronounced
dead.
It will all
come to that
and you
know it.
Your lies
will not
save you
or shield
you from
the consuming
black sun.
It is centuries of
lies which left
you here.
Make a friend
of the worm
a truer
soul mate
you will
never know.

Friends Of The Ex

When I meet them
I see that
she has filled them
with her *point of view*.
They stare and pout
at me from the edge
of their haunches
with absolute disgust.
One got so bold as to
call me from 300 miles away
to tell me what a *bum*
and piece of *shit*
I am. I listened for a few moments
trying to reason
with her, but finally I just hung up.
I sometimes
want to hate them in return
but I don't even hate the ex.
Though I am strangely
intimidated and
baffled by her continual
bizarre rage.
She has become like some crazy person
I don't care to know, like one of the
homeless
a complete stranger
screaming obscenities
at me
walking on the other
side of the street.

The True Story Of Noah

Several thousand years after the flood,
Noah parked the ark in the New York
harbor, got off to get a chili dog
at Nathan's
on Coney Island, took a cruise on the
Staten Island Ferry, and won 40 thousand
dollars in Atlantic City at the crap table. His wife, his sons,
and his son's wives were all still dead asleep
on the ark. Noah had drugged them with massive doses of
Pamelor, Vicodin, and Effexor so he could
get a little R&R, alone, without the
demands of domesticity. Everything was
beginning to annoy and outrage him on the ark. The daily rut
of keeping all the animals fed and clean, and all the shit
mopped up was a 24/7 job in itself; they had to do it
in 8 hour shifts. The constant bickering between the women
was becoming unbearable. And for the last
couple hundred years, his sons had developed
the bizarre habit of walking in on Noah and his wife,
      Mrs. Noah, when
they were drunk and fucking, which had caused
his wife not to get drunk and fuck
him, she just shut him off. Noah stayed away
from the ark for several weeks, going from
party to party at nights
and playing the stock market during the days. He came back
to the ark a rich and satisfied man, only to be
appalled by the fact that no one had made the slightest effort
to clean up the animal shit. He knew what had to be done and
threw himself right into it. When he was finished, there
was not a hint, a spot, a trace, or a whisper of
creature doo-doo. One clean ark, he determined! Then he
drugged them all again, fucked his sleeping wife, rented a car
      and drove to Hollywood, where
he is to this day contemplating that voice that
was booming from the sky thousands of years ago.

On The #41 Bus 3 a.m.

An old blind man
with a magnificent
pure white Malamute
told me, as he was
sitting down next to me, that he'd
just gotten off work
from his job as a
night watchman
at the Shell Oil building
downtown
then he yelled up
at the bus driver
asking
if I was smiling
and I was.

**Entertainment
(1920 to present)**

The guy who sat
2 seats
behind you
in the 10th
grade
who
could
fart louder
than anyone
in school.
The same guy who
came up
to you at
a high school
dance
and
brushed
his
fingers under
your nose
and
said:
"smell"
after
being
in the back
seat
with your ex-
girl friend.
This
guy
has
become
a
STAR:

writing
his
autobiography,
which is
being made
into a
movie
with him
starring.
He's
giving
interviews
about the
profundity
of his
popularity
and
on
a special
tv show
he came
flying
down from
the ceiling
on pulleys
and when
he landed
he farted
and huge
puffs
of smoke
and flames
shot
all
over
the stage.
There was
a French

guy
who
toured
all the
finest
theaters of
Europe
in the
1920's
who
could
blow out
candles
and
make
his
ass
talk
and sing
Parisian
lullabies
and
I bet
he
got
rich
and
got
a lot
of
pussy
too.

What She Wrote From Rural America

The moments dripped like frozen sap
down rusty pipes and the sky
chipped away like ancient paint from
motel walls. Her sons murdered
puppies and her husband ran
off with a 13 year old cotton candy twirler
from the county fair. The corn wouldn't grow
and the floods wiped out the future. She said madness
was her only refuge. She asked how I was doing
and if I was still married. I carefully resealed the
letter and wrote in bold across it:
deceased return to sender.

4th & Main

I sat behind the counter
always smoking something:
a cigarette, cigar, or
grass when I could get it.
There was a loaded shotgun
back there and
a cooler full of beer and
Pepsi and usually a pint of
Haig & Haig or Wild Turkey.
I'd spend the first 15 to 20
minutes of my shift
lining up the dildos by size
and sipping Pepsi and booze
from a paper cup
full of ice. The smallest one,
a 3 incher to the largest one,
14 inches. I'd line them all up
inside the counter to dick headed
perfection. I'd check the batteries
in the vibrators. People were always
asking me
to take
the vibrators out of the case
to see if they worked.
As people fondled and sized up
the plastic and rubber goods, I'd stand
and look out the window sipping my
drink and watching the sun set
in an expanding shadow over the brownstone
building across the street, which housed a
bar, a garment sweatshop, another porn shop,
and an Italian restaurant that had been
closed for many years

I heard that the former owners of the
the restaurant were followers

of Mussolini
and started the restaurant after he
was executed in 1943, and that
the waiters carried machine guns
under their
aprons. Some people believed the
stories, others didn't.
To me the stories were as real as anything; real as
the drunks, vice cops, junkies, speed freaks, alley sleeping
         homeless, and the sex freaks and the whores
walking in the front of, and walking in and out of
my place of employment.
Real as
the malnourished
Mexican kid
not more than 9 years old, coming in the store
and begging for change every other day. He'd
tell me I was his "mark," but
I didn't give a shit. Real as the rather foul breathed
man who asked me politely if I
would give him
head for $40. I sat my cup on the counter and
reached for the shotgun and stuck it
in his face. I looked at him closely
under the bright fluorescent light of the porn shop.
He had a face like a cocker spaniel
and pigeon eyes set close together and they
weren't focusing.
I lowered the shotgun gently back to its place next
to the cooler and pointed to the door.
The guy backed away with the look which had
frozen to his face when I pointed both barrels at him;
a look of such terror I pray I never see
on another human being again.

The machine gun carrying waiters
were real as the bus ride home

at 2 a.m. with the other night life workers: all
either stoned, sleeping or just bleary-eyed and exhausted.
The bus would travel
past the Mark Taper Forum
and over the freeway bridge into
Echo Park at the edge of
Chinatown
then up Sunset Boulevard to Silverlake
where I'd get off and walk up the
steep hill of Micheltorena to my court
apartment; to my sanctuary, my typewriter,
my freedom from insanity, from the
dire hopelessness of the streets.
I always paid my rent a couple months
in advance and the shades were always
drawn. As real as my fat Persian cat
waiting for me at the
door purring and screaming for food, real
as the 4 stucco walls which were
around me. I never doubted for a moment
that some of the doomed followers
of Mussolini opened a restaurant and
carried machine guns under their aprons
on the corner of 4th & Main.

Coltrane Mowing The Grass

Working up to the edge of my backyard
southeast corner facing California.
The mower spurting down the slope
weeping for oil, I catch
sight of the
chocolate brown short haired
cat from down
the street
dancing along
the fence. Coltrane is
playing on the disc player
from my open kitchen window.
And I turn off the mower and
sit down to watch the cat intently
my body full
of its supple moving and the rest of my senses
consumed by that
other cat, that dead cat, Coltrane.
My wife is yelling something at me from the porch
and our dog is barking at
the cat, but the cat dances
on, and that genius cat, John Coltrane,
wails and wails on and on. I go up on my porch to take
a break, my wife hands me an ice cold beer, and I
seriously consider hiring the kid next door
to finish mowing the grass, as I sit down, turn the music up,
close my eyes and throw the world
the finger.

Small Press Editor Gives Advice On How To Get Published In His Magazine

Write about
the fancy
shapes
you made
on roller
skates
when
you were
a kid, or

the color
of coffee
with cream
or without.
Mocha,
espresso, latte
whatever.

Write about
the pubic
hair
of the
woman
who broke
your heart, but

leave
the
social
concerns
to Oliver
Stone
and the
fucking
movies.

Leaving The Coast Of Georgia

She said she had
dreamt about leaving
the coast of
Georgia years
before she finally
did. Her last
job was at
Bell's Diner in
Atlanta, working
the grill and
serving the
counter. Her ex
was chasing
her around
making threatening
telephone calls
to Bell's
even when
she wasn't
there. Then her
daddy was found
dead in
a motel room
somewhere in
Maine with a $10
whore. His body
shipped home
by United Airlines.

Ginger Baker

she said that life
was a burning fuse
and she knew she'd
lose and I couldn't help her
anyway
she said this over
the pounding drums
of Ginger Baker
after we
dropped a lot
of acid
maybe 6 tabs
of windowpane
watching the orange sun set over downtown
Los Angeles
from the roof
of my house in
Echo Park
and the Dodgers were beating
the Giants
just over the hill in
Chavez Ravine and
I couldn't hear what she said
and i asked her
to repeat
it 4 times
the 4th time
her tears came and I
listened
closer

The Kid Guru From India

he was picking
his nose, which
put me off
right away.
he seemed to be
somewhat taken
back that
i was
not a follower. this
shocking fact
was
whispered to him
by the pretty girl
I came with
who was also his follower
(as he was picking
his nose). she
had brought me
there to meet him
and get converted
i suppose.
he stopped
smiling and
starting
humming
to himself.

she whispered
in my
ear then that
he was
doing his mantra.
another pretty
girl appeared
from nowhere
with some
bananas and

oranges in
a bowl. i
took an orange
and began
peeling it.
he stared at
me the
whole time
humming.
he finally spoke saying
the orange i
was peeling
and about
to digest
was like
the universe.
i took
a bite
of the orange
and said
it was
a real sweet
orange.

he began
rocking back
and forth
saying, "yes, yes, very good
yes, yes..."
almost
hysterically.
i looked around
for my
friend
remembering
that it was
nearly 6:30

and i was
missing
Jeopardy
on t.v.
as i was leaving
and explaining
the
urgency, he
seemed to
understand:
smiling and
nodding his
head, and
saying, "Jeopardy, Jeopardy
yes, yes"
and waving
goodbye
with his
nose-picking
hand.

Carnival Poem

it is useless to point out
the way grey
suddenly turned to brown
when I put my hand up her dress
between her thighs
and rubbed there
I say useless to point out because
when speaking of eyes
there are times when people
listen and they'll ask was I
sure her eyes were grey to begin with
when I put my hand up her dress
between her thighs
and rubbed there
or was I sure it was brown
they turned to not just a faded grey
well it wasn't just the eyes anyway
her whole face altered like a fun house mirror
and her voice took on the sound of
a faraway whirl and all I could hear
was the silhouette of her words
please do it harder please
bouncing off the water in
the Tunnel Of Love
when I put my hand up her dress
between her thighs
and rubbed there

On Elvis Presley's Birthday

Snow is falling heavy in
Oregon, right now, as it was doing
in Indiana that day when I was 13, when I
first heard Elvis sing *That's All Right, Mama*
at Joe's Record Shop on 2nd street.
The snow back then was in near blizzard
portions, as I
stood inside the store
listening and watching through the
storefront window
enormous flakes falling and
covering the sidewalk, street and cars
like a thick blanket being weaved.

But Presley disappointed me
when I saw his picture on
the sleeve that the record was in.
I had heard him singing before over the radio
from a station in Nashville
and he sounded like
a black man to me.
Elvis ain't
no name for a white man!
Though, as I continued to
listen to him, a certain kind of pride grew in me
for all of the mixed breeds of southern
and southern mid-western
white boys like ourselves
locked-up in one form or another of
grey and dingy poverty
living and dying in all of our
'heartbreak hotels.'

Now, 20 years after his death
it seems like the whole world, like the

Colonel, is selling him like a whore,
pimping him in the
lobbies of crass, cheap merchandise.
But back then it wasn't like
that. I carried that 45 RPM
record home
like it was a rare and priceless treasure.
Knowing within me it was a sign
of change in me, in music
in the world at large, in the universe of
perpetual movement and uncertainty.
Something was established that would change
everything forever.

Today, when I walk to my mailbox
in the snow, I see my footprints there, but on
that day when I was 13, I wouldn't
have been surprised to have looked
and seen only snow.

Sometimes

sometimes it points to the sky
of blue pointing like a bird
dog. sometimes it buries itself
deep in the nothingness
of political thinking. sometimes
it screams through the black
black lies once told by you
and I. sometimes it just sits
there like J.Edgar Hoover
with a cheap tape recorder
plotting your death. sometimes
it spends years adding up numbers
in an attempt to round off
infinity. sometimes it hides
in the couch with change
from 100's of pockets.
sometimes it burns and burns
the trees we can't see the
forest for. sometimes
it runs like an out of control
driver-less locomotive down a
steep mountain pass.
sometimes it stands trendy poets
up against the wall of
timeless literature and shoots them.
sometimes it lances boils on the
butts of opossums. sometimes it checks
into motels under the names of
Curly, Moe and Larry. sometimes it
loves beauty for the right reasons.
sometimes it can name every
painting in the Chicago Art Museum
blindfolded. sometimes it is impossible
to decode with extra sensory perception
or any other kind of perception.
sometimes it breaks your heart. sometimes

it plans wars on planets in
distant galaxies. sometimes it
whittles exquisite little angels
out of cherry wood. sometimes it stands on
its head and imitates Erica Jong.
sometimes it captures butterflies
then sets them free in the Pope's
bedroom. sometimes it goes into
tirades over the absurdity of
collective consciousness. sometimes it
teaches law students at Harvard how to make
tiny gas chambers. sometimes it stumbles around
in Dante's *Inferno* selling copies of
Milton's *Paradise Lost*. sometimes it poses
as P.T. Barnum standing behind
a billboard trying to explain the difference
between propaganda and advertising.
sometimes it wishes on a star. sometimes
it pretends to be a tug boat on the
Mississippi in 1859. sometimes it's
a relief. sometimes it surfaces
in London claiming it never knew
the gun was loaded. sometimes it
whirls like a ballet
dancer in the middle of
a completely empty Times
Square. sometimes it simply
is not there regardless of what
blind faith may say. sometimes
it counts all the hairs on your
head then splits them. sometimes
it can be caught adjusting the
color control on the telescope at
the Griffith Observatory.
sometimes it
peters out before you do. sometimes
it gets solar activity

to disrupt tv transmissions. sometimes
it resembles a dove
flying above. sometimes it shoots out
street lights.
sometimes it never never stands
in a certain place overlooking
the Hudson river. sometimes it
has no remorse. sometimes it shines!
sometimes it rolls around in history.
sometimes it's as lonely as a
grave. sometimes it sky dives in
the Grand Canyon. sometimes it
can be heard giving a testimony on true
love at the Taj Mahal. sometimes it takes
pictures of fat men eating. sometimes
it fastens itself on the
back of poor judgment. sometimes it holds to
truths that are self evident. sometimes it wanders
around in the wilderness for 40 years missing
the way out repeatedly. sometimes it's out of
focus. sometimes it has no reason
for being. sometimes it foams at the
mouth then spits up into oblivion. sometimes
it hammers invisible nails into
smog. sometimes it simply is! sometimes it
sets a course for Easter Island. sometimes
it walks the floors at Graceland. sometimes
it has a way of fooling the wisest of men.
sometimes it leaks information to
expired newspapers. sometimes it
has no way of coping. sometimes it
circles the covered wagons. sometimes it knows no
limits. sometimes it climbs mountains
dressed in a tuxedo. sometimes it
is released from bondage. sometimes it is
functional for a few minutes.
sometimes it divides nations.

sometimes it
shimmers on the moonlit water. sometimes it runs a
race with stolen shoes. sometimes it pauses
for applause. sometimes it deals cards
from the bottom of the deck. sometimes it alters
events for diabolical purposes. sometimes it is
your friend. sometimes it jumps like a
jack rabbit into the red moon. sometimes it moves
around the bases like a 90 year old Babe Ruth.

Sincere Foolishness Is Rewarded With Nothing

Nights in Chicago
at 19
writing bleeding
letters to other
poets for
camaraderie. I never
received any
answers.
Days in '68 on the
streets of L.A.
sending a book of
poems to City Lights
with a half-ass
suicide note (if they didn't publish me
                I was gonna
          jump off the San Bernardino
               freeway bridge
                      onto
             Crenshaw Boulevard).
They didn't publish it of course
sent it back a year
after I'd decided to jump and pieces of me
scattered to the far corners. My left leg made it to the outskirts
          of San Diego, my cock & large hairy balls
got it as far as Reno (go figure)
my heart was found in a gravel parking lot
in front of Millie's Beer & Suds
in Riverside
looking like the corpse of Ezra Pound.

Sally

I couldn't tell whether she was
a man or woman at first. I took the
bottle anyway. It was four in the morning
and the rain was beginning to fall
as we huddled together in the alley off of
5th and Temple in downtown L.A. The Night
Train was smooth going down warming my throat and
stomach. After passing the bottle back and forth
a few times, I found out her name was Sally.
She was younger than me; she took off her Cincinnati
Reds baseball cap and her hair was matted and
filthy, but through it all, a radiant shiny black.

She asked if I wanted some sex. I told her no, I was
too tired for that. She seemed relieved but shot me a
quick disgusted look. "You're not a fag, are you?"
she asked. "No," I answered, "just real tired."
Sally was from Baltimore. Had been living on the streets
for over a year, and when she couldn't stand it
any longer, the women's shelter at the mission.

Her father raped her.
Her brother raped her.
Her uncle raped her.
Her mother broke her arm and called her a whore
         throwing her out on the streets when she
was 16. "The fucking world sucks," she said. I nodded in
agreement, taking another long pull from the bottle.

We sat huddled, talking together till the rain stopped
and the sun was breaking out over the downtown
skyline. Pigeons flew in the morning light overhead.
I left her there about 6 a.m. sleeping up against a cardboard
garment box, and headed back to my apartment in Silverlake.

It'd been 3 long days of booze, speed, weed,

debauchery, madness, lies and violence. Little
of which I remember, but I do remember
waking up in that stinking alley
next to her warmth, with no hope but the bottle
no desire but to warm myself, no thoughts
no future.
As I walked out of the alley onto 5th street I
looked back at her sleeping peacefully
and in the light and fading shadows of
morning she was almost beautiful.

After these many years of my life, of drugs, booze,
marriage, poetry, divorce, love, resurrection,
friendships, poverty, prosperity, death, homelessness,
children, betrayal, rage, faith; the endless nowhere shit-hole jobs
and all the rest of the moments
which brought me to the moment of this memory
my tears saturate the paper for Sally
and I raise my fist to the world
for her, myself and all the rest of you.

Molly's Place

Back when bebop had overcome me and
rockabilly was not that far behind, in the summer
of my 15th year on this earth, Charlie
and I spent most of our afternoons down at
Molly's place: a "colored" whore house on
the other side of the B&O railroad tracks in
Vincennes, Indiana. We'd sit under her big sycamore
tree listening to the jukebox sounds of Muddy Waters,
Howlin' Wolf, Billie Holiday, and Lead Belly coming
from her screened in porch, where her johns
waited for the pretty young black girls. Oh, what soul jarring
sounds they were!

But at school, we both cringed under the desks after films on
the H-bomb that were shown between films on
dental hygiene. What tooth decay had to do with total
annihilation of the human race, I have yet
to understand. I would much rather have been down
at Molly's with Charlie listening to the throbbing sounds
of real life.

Molly spoke to us only twice, though she
must've passed us a 100 times. We were always
trying to melt into the tree. "What you
boys doin' out here?" she asked. I
told her we were just listening to the music.
She laughed. Her laugh was strong and
open. The only other time she spoke was when she
was fuming at one of the girls inside. She stormed
down the steps of the house and down the walk
passing us behind the tree. "Hope music
is all you boys hearin'."

One day that 15th summer, Charlie died
in a fall from his bike, head first onto a concrete slab
that his mother hung the clothes out to dry over.

His brother, a few days before, had found
Charlie and I sitting under that sycamore
tree. He yelled at us about "niggers" and
disease. Charlie just blinked and followed him
home. My dad, drunk one day, asked me where I was spending
my afternoons. I could do nothing but lie. A few days later
at the funeral, I helped carry Charlie's casket; a
pallbearer for a weird white kid like me, who liked
music and young black girls.

The next day after the funeral, I was back at Molly's
sitting under the tree. She came out
smiling sadly and handed me a plate of the best
peanut butter cookies I've ever eaten. I ate four of the ten
cookies in honor of Charlie later that night as I listened
to Little Richard over the radio from Nashville. I rocked out
moving into my darkened room in a frenzy... with tears I am
not ashamed of, and with laughter that was like the tooth decay
and the bomb, something else I will never understand.

Trip To Nowhere

Where I found answers I
could not find questions
for. The middle was not
in the middle but off
to the right side, positioned
like an open grave. Voices
spoke in English making
no grammatical sense. I
grabbed hold of
the edge
of something freezing and fierce
which took off all my flesh up
to my elbow. There was no moon
or sun or stars or sky
only rain and movement all
around me like
speeding trains on
rusty tracks. No entrance, no
exit, no way of telling light
from dark. My bones
broke like pencils
against monolithic structures everywhere
I turned
and everywhere was nowhere
and somewhere was slaughtered with
no purpose and no direction.
Suddenly there was a sound like
millions
of breaking windows
smashing in echo chambers
over and over. I knew then, somehow, I had broken
through and that my bones would
heal. I would form new skin on
my arm, and the questions were something
in the middle once again. The moon, the
sun, the stars and the sky were
there too.

Now That You Are Gone
for Beth

The fact that we can receive
and transmit
music and voices through the air
amazes me. Everything amazes me!
That life goes on amazes me. Your body
is under the
earth now. Molecules still expand
and contract. People are still at
war: the couple up front are still
trying to
kill each other. Children born innocent
still have a chance, if they don't
accept it all. You are gone. Wall
Street goes on. Flowers grow.
They still pick up the garbage. Evil
people who should have died
long ago still suck blood.
It all amazes me! My love
for you and your love
for me always amazed me.
And I pray your spirit
finds rest from
the world that killed
you.
What I want to know is where can I offer
myself up? What mountain do I climb?

Rural American Saga

His mommy
told him
to take
daddy's
shot gun
and shoot
daddy in
the stomach
with one
barrel and
shoot him
in the head
with the
other
barrel.

He did as
his mommy
told him
and he
watched the
blood sputter
with the first
shot to
daddy's
stomach
and he
watched his daddy
clutch his
stomach, falling
onto the kitchen table.

He aimed
and shot his
daddy's head

and watched
his daddy's
brains splash out
on the black & white
checkered
linoleum.

His mommy
helped him
drag his
daddy's
conscious
but barely
alive body out
to the
barnyard
where mommy
stabbed his
daddy with a
hunting knife
20 times—
one for every
year of their
marriage

5 Portraits Of Downtown Los Angeles

1.
He looked like
        General
de Gaulle.
Wore
       dresses
                        & hung around 6th & Main
with
      his
hand out like a rusty pump handle.
                     Heavy sweat
                           pouring dirt through
                                yesterday's make-up.

2.
Hair like a mop, black in color.
               Banging his head on the side of the Bank of
                        America building on
    7th & Spring
& pulling his hair
                in the same motion.
& as we pass
               we have to lean
                       close to hear him ask
    in a whisper,
              " gotta quarter, gotta quarter."

3.
With a back
               the size of a Main Street doorway.
    Black patch over his left eye
                     with a star shaped diamond
        in the middle.
Cursing under his breath, "mudafucka, mudafucka,
                         you mudafucka."

4.
She sleeps near a taco stand off the
corner of
6th & Hill
on two green garbage bags which contain
her entire possessions.
She smells like the Chicago
stockyards.
One morning I offered her a cup of
coffee & a donut & she
spat at me & made a hissing
sound like a curled up garden hose full of water
building to the nozzle.

5.
Screaming down the middle of
6th street
between Broadway & Hill.
Dodging around the cars like a runaway
slave– a white slave, at that, with long red hair.
He was bleeding
down his cheek.
Two cops
with guns drawn
were chasing him
breathing like a box springs.

Boiling Eggs

a freckled face kid brings
a new telephone book
to my
open
door

i don't have a phone

my wife is flipping thru an
old copy of *Captain Marvel*
she looks up & smiles at him
tells him we
don't have a phone
goes into detail
about the phone being taken out
for failure
to pay the bill

i'm boiling eggs in the kitchen

her & the kid come in to watch me pour
the boiling water down the drain
while gingerly
lifting each
one of the
4 eggs out
with a spoon
like sleeping infants
from a crib

Pretending The Apple Pie Is Fresh

Pretending what can only be pretended
in the hollow cave of
a diseased mind and laughing
like a crater on the moon: dead and
deep and treacherous.

War mongers and whore mongers
dine with presidents and kings
on lavish tables.

Meteors and broken stars are buried
beneath the junkyards of the world.
Dignity is something sold on back streets
and in dark crevices.

No matter how often flowers wither and
die in the presence of politicians
no matter what the earth is destined to
spew out of its bowels, no matter what price
the death of innocence
the horror continues unchecked by the
appointed and elected guardians of society.

Legions march heads-up past the viewing stand
where the decked-out
dignitaries are seated with chests full of medals
wearing thousand dollar suits, their wives
smiling beside them
like vampy Vegas whores.

Time Travel

Pass me the DNA
sneak over and chop off a good sized
atom with the proton, neutron, and
electron intact.

Dig up a 15th century sundial
watched over in Constantine's court.
Sift through the sand for a
perfect grain from the
banks of the Euphrates river.

Please, don't strap me down with anything
electronic or computerized.
Just feed me bananas for the potassium and
massive dozes of vitamin C, E, and B-12.

Read me all of Einstein's dairies
while standing on your head.

Find me the exact Hebrew translation
for the word "chromosome."

Turn your watch backward precisely 3 hours
16 1/2 minutes and 3 seconds.

Look up a sanctified usher to lead me to the
outside corridor of the inner chamber.

And have a 1947 Pittsburgh streetcar waiting at
the other end
stocked full of ice cold beer, fresh sour cream
and hot potato latkes.

Bird Watching At Burger King

He looked at me and I
looked at him. He knew
that I knew the score as his
wild-haired bovine wife wiped down
a table at Burger King
yelling at 2 small children
and barking at him
I'm going to the crapper
watch the kids
our number is 23!
I turned away but I could
feel his eyes on me as I watched
a beautiful blue bird
outside eating a
crumb of a hamburger bun
with perfect
dignity.

Worker 1943-46

He had Churchill's face
and Hitler's body
standing behind a
a poster of Roosevelt
(in his wheelchair). I
was just born
on the
other
side of the
world. My daddy
drove a *Willy's*
panel wagon. They
were bombing
London and bombing
Indiana gravel pits
for the sport
and telling lies
to their priests. He was
pouring
liquid
steel
from huge vats, drinking
Old Grand Dad
by the gallon and
breaking the hearts
of truck stop whores
who had
brothers and husbands
dying overseas
for all of us.

Colors And Other Things

the blues were blue
and the reds were not
quite as red as I
had remembered   but you
looked the same as you
always looked I suppose
and you still were pretentious
as hell when saying love
love love like it was a
leaching sickness and you
called me a pet name
you used to use when we
were pretending a life
together   a love together
and your fingers were ice
cold when you touched my
back and I tensed and you noticed
and perhaps (somewhat)
you became aware of the present
and your lousy color contrast
and that love is not need
need is not love love love
and time passes   things
end others begin new love
new heart   your heart
is the same old heart   bleeds
like an ulcer and I
can't stop the bleeding
and I never could

Coming Full Cycle

The men move like morgue
attendants
while the women flirt and bake pies
for the county fair.

The skeletons in their
closets dance a
jig to
mediocrity.

War veteran sons come home in pieces
or sort of
alive in body
but dead in the head.

What more can they give
than what they've already given up?

Crimes of betrayal and government
blackmail
weave through the crumbling fabric of
American life.

The government stopped being honorable when
they started butchering Indians
and stealing their land.

Now the crops from the land will not pay the mortgages
of decent people who
never butchered anything
except food to eat or sell.

Living Off The Land

Nothing changes. The
directions blew away
in the tornado. Music
plays on the radio but
is turned so low
you can't tell whether it's
Ernest Tubbs
or Willie Nelson.
The cat sleeps under
the bath tub
curled up on an old copy
of Time Magazine: one
with Richard Nixon
on the cover. A farmer
down the road shot
his wife his brother-in-law
and himself. Neighbors
bring food to the 18 year
old surviving son.
The grandfather clock
on the wall
is 3 years old
won in a Kroger
grocery store
raffle. The t.v. set gets
150 channels all with
fuzzy vertical hold.

Scenes

10:00 a.m.
Rommel lying in the hospital
talking about Hitler's
hysterics "the screaming &
weeping of a high strung
woman."

1:30 p.m.
Gary Cooper looks puzzled
about a bug on his
sleeve. Gary Cooper
looks puzzled
on a horse but the
bug is gone.

4:03 p.m.
Vittorio De Sica bumps his
nose on Marlene Dietrich's
necklace; outside three servants
bend over the keyhole like
one giant praying mantis.

Dream After Reading The 3 Little Pigs To A Bored 4 Year Old On The Beach At Venice

The window was open wide & 3 faces were staring out at me. I knew one of them was a bookie from Chicago named Frankco, a face from my past, that I'd once ran numbers for when I was 18. The other 2 were friends of Frankco, or so it seemed: Frankco was in the middle & the other 2 had their arms around him, they were all wearing shit-eating grins.

The house was an English Tudor, a beautiful job with vines curling up all around it. It sat so close to the ocean, at high tide the back porch was covered with a foot of water.

I sat there on the sand with little Calvin trying to figure it all out. Knowing that Frankco was bad karma to the max. I told little Calvin to look at *this* & then I took several deep breaths, huffed & puffed & blew the fucking house down.

What Kind Of Bird Was It

Burned up & dead is
a bird on my front step.
The bird was put there
partly burned there
by the 7 year old
next door.

He hates me because I
have more women
than him— who walk up my walk
playing with the cats
& smiling at him.

He would love to cream my guts out
with a flame torch.
The women are fascinated by him.
I tell them: no, he's a vicious
little bastard.

They just smile & ask
me sweetly "What kind of
bird was it?"

Odds

There is no way
in the world to
settle with it
no tight rational
explanation to
satisfy all that
ignorant and dead
conventional
thought.

The fact
is, dice have a
predicable
ratio only in
relation to where
and how they're
being thrown.

Even if they're thrown
hard and against
iron clad walls
for half a century...

It's then you see
the crushing odds
and you know
you have
beaten them.
Somehow. You know
with the certainty
of your continued
breath.

Doug Draime has been a presence in the underground literary movement since the late 1960's. He lives in Ashland, Oregon with wife and family.

Grateful acknowledgment is made to the editors and publishers of the numerous magazines, anthologies, and journals where many of these poems have appeared.

The author also wishes a special thanks to the editors of the following chapbooks where some of these poems were published: *Unoccupied Zone* (**Pitchfork Press**), *Spit Madmen* (**Scintillating Publications**), *Eyestone* (**Kendra Steiner Editions**), *Knox County* (**Kendra Steiner Editions**), *Rock 'n Jizz* (**Propaganda Press**), and *Los Angeles Terminal: Poems 1971-1980* (**Covert Press**).

www.ingramcontent.com/pod-product-compliance
Lightning Source LLC
Chambersburg PA
CBHW020937090426
42736CB00010B/1173